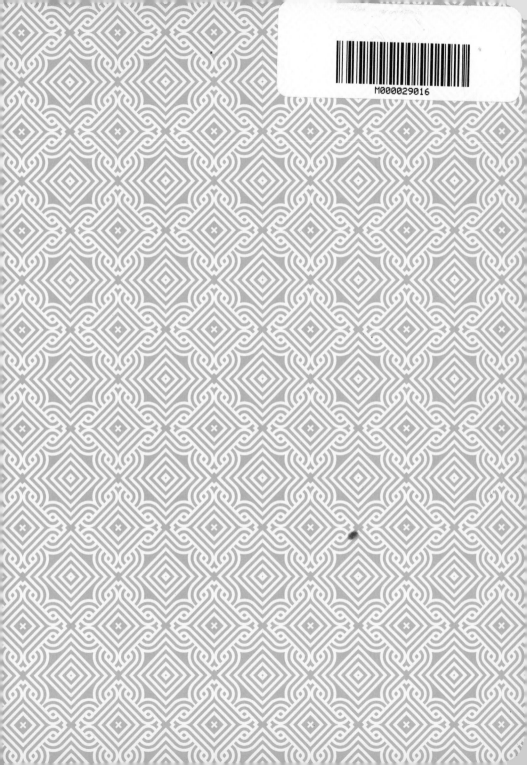

This journal belongs to

....

$\mathcal{C}$ourage is contagious. When a brave person takes a stand,
the spines of others are often stiffened.

BILLY GRAHAM

*Y*ou are a beloved child of God, precious to Him in every way. As you seek Him, He will show you the mysteries of life and unfold His unique plans for you—a life full of rich blessing and peaceful assurance. God cares about you and knows all the desires of your heart. He is as close as breathing.

Let this journal inspire you to express your thoughts, record your prayers, embrace your dreams, and listen to what God is saying to you. Be brave. You are not in this alone.

2:45 - 2:50 - what are you doing?

2:50 - 2:55 - sample pantomimes &
                breaking into groups

3:00 - 3:25 - Designing pantomimes

Occupations	Locations
✓ Doctor	- The Beach
✓ = Lifeguard	- Outer Space ✓
✓ - Farmer	- Disneyland
- Teacher	- The movies
- Actor	- The zoo
- Rockstar	- An arcade ✓
- Spy	- Coffee Shop ✓
- Chef	- A park
- Model	

Wed 11th

#33325093

$\mathcal{T}$here will always be the unknown. There will always be the unprovable.
But faith confronts those frontiers with a thrilling leap.
Then life becomes vibrant with adventure!

ROBERT SCHULLER

I can do all things through Christ who strengthens me.

THE BIBLE

_A_ hero is no braver than an ordinary person.
A hero simply holds on to courage a few minutes longer.

*B*e still, and in the quiet moments, listen to the voice of your heavenly Father. His words can renew your spirit...no one knows you and your needs like He does.

JANET L. SMITH

*L*ive as brave people; and if fortune is adverse,
front its blows with brave hearts.

MARCUS TULLIUS CICERO

_G_od may be invisible, but He's in touch. You may not be able to see Him, but He is in control. And that includes you—your circumstances. That includes what you've just lost. That includes what you've just gained. That includes all of life—past, present, future.

CHARLES R. SWINDOLL

Let us come boldly to the throne of our gracious God. There we will receive his mercy, and we will find grace to help us when we need it most.

THE BIBLE

*C*ourage isn't a feeling that you wait for. Courage is doing
when you don't have courage. Courage is doing it scared.

JILL BRISCOE

Whatever the circumstances, whatever the call...
His strength will be your strength in your hour of need.

BILLY GRAHAM

*Courage might not be about bravery or doing something worthy
of valor. Courage, sometimes, might just be being present.*

SARAH MARKLEY

*O*utside our comfort zone...
is where we experience the true awesomeness of God.

LYSA TERKEURST

*G*od is our refuge and strength, an ever-present help in trouble.
Therefore we will not fear.

THE BIBLE

O Lord...let me not fear too much the storms and winds of my daily life,
and let me know that there is ebb and flow...but that the sea remains the sea.

HENRI J. M. NOUWEN

*G*od does not change, but He uses change—to change us. He sends us on journeys that bring us to the end of ourselves. We often feel out of control, yet if we embrace His leading, we may find ourselves on the ride of our lives.

JEN HATMAKER

*C*ourage is not about knowing the path. It is about taking the first step.

KATIE J. DAVIS

*W*atch, stand fast in the faith, be brave, be strong.

THE BIBLE

*The weaker I am, the harder I must lean on God's grace;
the harder I lean on Him, the stronger I discover Him to be,
and the bolder my testimony to His grace.*

JONI EARECKSON TADA

_W_hen you believe God is who He says He is, when you hang onto Him and His Word in faith, His truth sets you free. The truth you store up in silence comes back to you in the storm, and it lifts you away as on a life raft from the fears and disappointments that would otherwise pull you down.

CHRISTINE CAINE

*G*od wants you to get where God wants you to go more
than you want to get where God wants you to go.

MARK BATTERSON

*W*ait patiently for the LORD. Be brave and courageous.
Yes, wait patiently for the LORD.

THE BIBLE

I learned that courage was not the absence of fear, but the triumph over it.
The brave person is not one who does not feel afraid, but one who conquers that fear.

NELSON MANDELA

....

....

....

....

....

....

....

....

....

....

....

....

....

....

....

....

....

....

....

....

When God speaks, oftentimes His voice
will call for an act of courage on our part.

CHARLES STANLEY

*K*eep your face to the sunshine and you cannot see a shadow.
HELEN KELLER

I love those who can smile in trouble,
who can gather strength from distress, and grow brave by reflection.

LEONARDO DA VINCI

*L*eave it all in the hands that were wounded for you.

ELISABETH ELLIOT

_H_ave courage for the great sorrows of life and patience for the small ones.
And when you have finished your daily task, go to sleep in peace. God is awake.

VICTOR HUGO

*The only use of an obstacle is to be overcome. All that an obstacle does with brave people is, not to frighten them, but to challenge them.

WOODROW WILSON

*I*t is God who arms me with strength, and makes my way perfect.

THE BIBLE

Not reaching back for what was lost in my yesterdays. And not reaching for what I hope will be in my tomorrow. But living fully with what is right in front of me. And truly seeing the gift of this moment.

LYSA TERKEURST

Ellie Claire® Gift & Paper Expressions
Franklin, TN 37067
EllieClaire.com
Ellie Claire is a registered trademark of Worthy Media, Inc.

Be Brave Journal
© 2016 by Ellie Claire
Published by Ellie Claire, an imprint of Worthy Publishing Group,
a division of Worthy Media, Inc.

ISBN 978-1-63326-119-8

Stock or custom editions of Ellie Claire titles may be purchased in bulk for educational,
business, ministry, fundraising, or sales promotional use. For information, please e-mail
info@EllieClaire.com

Compiled by Jill Jones
Cover art © Shutterstock | www.shutterstock.com
Printed in China

1 2 3 4 5 6 7 8 9 – 21 20 19 18 17 16